HOW TO GET UP WHEN SCHOOLWORK GETS YOU DOWN

Claudine G. Wirths, M.A. & Mary Bowman-Kruhm, Ed.D.

CHARIOT
FAMILY PUBLISHING

Chariot Books™ is an imprint of David C. Cook Publishing Co.
David C. Cook Publishing Co., Elgin, Illinois 60120
David C. Cook Publishing Co., Weston, Ontario
Nova Distribution Ltd., Newton Abbot, England

HOW TO GET UP WHEN SCHOOLWORK GETS YOU DOWN

Designed by Foster Design
Cover and interior illustrations by Corey Wilkinson
First Printing, 1993
Printed in the United States of America
97 96 95 94 93 5 4 3 2 1

Library of Congress Cataloging-in-Publication Data
Wirths, Claudine G.
How to get up when schoolwork gets you down/Claudine G. Wirths, Mary Bowman-Kruhm.
p. cm.
ISBN 0-7814-0118-6
1. Study, Method of—Juvenile literature. 2. Homework—Juvenile literature.
I. Bowman-Kruhm, Mary. II. Title.
LB1049.W57 1993 93-3050
371.3'028'12—dc20 CIP
AC

HOMEWORK!

Hello there! Glad you could take the time to talk with us today. As teachers, we see a lot of young people like you—young people who are plenty smart, who want to do well in school, and who are willing to work hard. But, while some of you seem to be born students, others of you find getting great grades is really hard.

Boy, that's me!
You are not alone! We have some ideas to help you with your schoolwork and we'd like to share them with you. Want to give our ideas a try?

I don't think they're going to work!
Come on. What have you got to lose?

A whole afternoon at the mall, that's what!
If our ideas work for you, doing your schoolwork will be easier and you'll find you have a lot more time

for going to the mall, talking with friends, and doing other things. Better yet, you won't have to feel guilty because you aren't doing as well in school as you know you can. If our ideas don't work for you, you can always go back to doing things the old way. Fair enough?

I guess so.
Let's start by talking about the word no one wants to hear—homework!

Yuk! I really hate homework. I don't know why teachers give us so much.
A lot of your peers feel the same way. The truth is that teachers know students have to practice and practice to get facts fixed in their memory. There just isn't enough time in a school day to learn all you have to know to be well educated. God has given you the power to learn, and you must use it or lose it.

That makes sense, but I wish someone would invent a smart pill that could make me learn without all that practice, practice.
No pills will ever substitute for your wonderful God-given brains. So why don't we begin by looking at how you plan your homework time.

What's to plan? I open up the first book on top of my desk and start. Planning would just take up more of my time.
No way! A plan will save you time. It will help you

get organized to do your studying as quickly and correctly as possible. Since everyone has a different study style, it is important that you decide on a plan that works best for you and the way you learn. Begin by asking yourself three questions:

- •What's my most important subject?
- •What's the best subject for me to start on?
- •What homework should I do last or not at all?

"Not at all"! You mean I don't have to do all my homework every day?
You should do all your homework every day, but DO you always do it?

I've got to admit—I don't always. If my mom is late getting home from work, I have to fix dinner and clean up. Then if I call some friends on the phone, I don't always have time to finish everything before I go to bed.
So what gets left till last or stays undone?

Just whatever I didn't get to.
That's why you need a plan. You should do all of your homework every day, but plan to do your most important assignments first. Then you can be sure to finish the ones that matter. If you don't finish because of an emergency, you can catch up the next day.

How do I know what's the most important class? Every teacher acts as if his or hers is the most important one.

Right. And that's the way all teachers should think about their subject. But by most important, we mean the class that is most important to you. What is the subject you need to spend time on if you're going to keep up your grades? What class do you need to work hardest on?

Do you mean like math? I hardly ever do well in math.
Exactly! If doing math homework is the most important thing to work on to keep your grade up, plan to do it every day when you are at your best.

There's no way I could make myself do math every day. It's so hard and so boorring!
Yes, you can. When you have real trouble doing a hard job, remember that God has given you the power to do what's best for you. Begin your math homework with a short prayer for strength. See if that doesn't help.

I never thought of that. That might help once I get started. But I have a hard time starting at all.
Same for us! Instead of sitting right down to grade papers, we find ourselves getting a snack or sharpening pencils or taking the dog for a walk.

So how do you finally get started?
Since some small tasks are easier to do, maybe like putting the papers in order, we warm up with that. Maybe you could start with looking up vocabulary

words for history. Once you get started, you'll find it's easier to keep going. When your brain is in gear, go right to your most important or hardest homework.

But suppose I don't have any simple stuff to do?
Say to yourself, "If I were going to do just ten minutes of homework now, what subject would I do?" Set a timer for ten minutes. Then work on that subject for just ten minutes. When the buzzer sounds, you'll find that it is easy to keep on working.

Even after I get started I have another problem. My friends are always calling me on the phone when I'm studying. They don't spend half as much time on homework as I do and their grades are better than mine. I wish I could be as smart as they are.
Don't be too hard on yourself. God has reasons for making us all different. You are special in your own way. Ask your friends not to call you, but tell them you'll call just as soon as you finish your work. A true friend will understand that you have to put schoolwork first.

My mom makes me do my homework at the same time every day. She asked me when I wanted to do it, so I chose right after dinner and after my half hour of TV. I'm too tired when I get home from school. I'd like to watch more TV, but she won't let me.

Good for your mom! Setting a time for homework every day is absolutely necessary. Doing homework should be like brushing your teeth—something you do every day at a certain time in a certain place without having to think about it.

Also be sure you have all the supplies you'll need before you start: a dictionary and thesaurus, some notebook paper, and a pen and pencil. You may need special supplies, like tracing paper, a compass or calculator, a ruler, and markers. You wouldn't want to look all over the house for your toothbrush every time, would you?

That sounds dumb, but I know what you mean. I waste a lot of time looking for stuff. Maybe I could put all my school things in a box. I could keep the box where I can always find it . . . and my little brother can't!

Right! School is your job. You need to look at it just the way you would if you ran a small business. You need a special time to go to work, and your brother shouldn't be allowed to bother you during your work time or mess around with your supplies ever. Ask your mom for help if your brother doesn't understand.

I like the idea of homework being a business. Maybe I'll set up an "office" in the basement and keep my box of school stuff there.
Good idea. That means we need to talk about keeping track of your business, too. To do that, use some kind of assignment sheet every day.

Aw, not that! Assignment sheets are for someone in trouble. I remember having to carry one of those around once. All my teachers had to sign it, and so did my parents. No way do I want to do that again!
Remember? This is your business. Every businessman or businesswoman keeps track of appointments and when to meet with clients. You need some kind of an assignment sheet you can flip right to in every class. The front or back of your notebook is a logical place to keep it.

You don't have to use a school assignment sheet unless your teachers say you have to. Look in the back of this book and you will see some samples we made up. Use ours, if you want to. We left room for doodles and dates for all the important things in your life as well as homework. There's a special place too, for keeping track of long-range projects.

Transfer those long-range dates to a big calendar near your desk. You don't want to miss a party because you forgot to finish a science report on time.

Isn't there anything else I can use besides an assignment sheet? They really are a pain.

Some people find they can use those note pads with a sticky edge on the back. They write homework assignments on them, one to a subject, and stick them on the book needed for that homework.

No matter which system you use, you'll have a good sense of accomplishment. When all the work you've jotted on the sticky notes is done, the notes can be tossed away. People who use assignment sheets get a feeling of success by checking off each assignment when they finish it.

I like the idea of using sticky notes—especially trashing them. But I have another problem. It may sound dumb, but I forget to take in homework after I've done it, or I can't find it after I get to school.

Lots of people have that problem. As you go farther in school, you will find that you have more and more papers to deal with. If you just throw them in your backpack, the homework you do in October may not surface until June!

You need a way to keep track of them, a system that works for you. Find what works for your best friend, or ask older students what works for them. Keep in mind that what works for others may not be right for you. Check out office supply stores and variety stores. Try several ways until you find your way.

Here are some ideas you can try, but we bet you can think of lots more:

- Use a different kind of notebook—one that has side pockets and special sections for each subject.
- Use a set of colored folders with pockets in them—a different color for each subject. Keep unfinished homework on one side. As soon as you have finished it, move it to the other side.
- Or use several three-ring binders, again with a different color binder for each subject. Tape a large paper or plastic envelope in the front of each one for homework due the next day.

Whatever system you find best, every day put all of your materials in your backpack. Then you'll know where everything is. Remember: your goal is to find a way of organizing papers that makes sense to you and the way your mind works.

But what about remembering to take library books or notes from my parents back to school?
Use a "tweaker."

A WHAT?
A tweaker. That's what we call it. Put something like a paper clip in a shoe the night before. The next morning when you stick your foot in the shoe, the paper clip "tweaks" your brain. Right away you remember that special project.

That's cool! Could I use a dog biscuit?
Sure, if it's okay with your dog.

Well, what do you think? Do you have some better ideas now on how to go about doing homework?

You bet. I can't wait to find a tweaker! . . . But it doesn't change the way I feel about doing homework. I still think it spoils my day.
A homework plan won't change the way you feel about homework. Only you can change the way you feel about anything. Maybe you should think about changing the way you look at homework. We don't expect you to love it, but we do know that as long as you feel that you hate it, you'll be miserable every day.

Ask God to help you try harder at school. Do your part by making a personal promise to yourself to make a homework plan and try to keep it. We promise that then you'll begin to feel better about yourself and homework. Soon homework will be just another job you do—not something that you let make your life miserable.

I would like to feel better about myself. Maybe I'll try it your way for a change.
Not OUR way. Remember, do it YOUR best way, and we know you'll do just fine. Next time let's talk about how we can help you with your work in math.

THE PROBLEM OF MATH

How are you doing with your homework plan?

I've thought a lot about finding my own way to do schoolwork. But there's no way I can do math. It's just too hard for me. Some of my friends seem to get it without even trying.

Simply accept the strengths and needs each of us has as part of God's plan. Here are three ways to remind you of the strengths God gave you:

- Think of the things you have done or made or said that you are proud of.
- Think of what you were doing when people patted you on the back and said, "Good job!"
- Ask people who are close to you what you do well.

I guess I am good at doing lots of things, but I still say I'm hopeless in math.

You can learn to do math well enough to meet what your school requires, your parents expect, and you hope for—if you work at it one step at a time. Building your skills in math is like building a house. You can't build a house by starting with the second floor. You first have to build a solid foundation.

I know what the foundation of a house is. What do you mean by foundation when it comes to math?

By having a solid foundation, we mean that you know how to add, subtract, multiply, and divide accurately without even having to think about how to do it. You have to know why as well as how you do the process that will give you the right answer. You also need to know your multiplication tables through the twelves so the answers come automatically. If you don't yet have those skills, work on them until you do. Set aside a time every day to practice your math skills, over and above your assigned work.

I guess if I spent more time on math I would do better in it.

Extra time is not the whole answer. Working at something the wrong way can make even more trouble for you. Be absolutely sure you understand and know how to do a basic math process before you move on. In math you have to understand every step as you take it. Ask your teacher to help if you don't understand both the how and the why of each step.

Our teacher gets us started on our homework in class and I think I'll be able to do it. Then when I sit down at home I forget how. What should I do then?

Ask yourself questions like these:

- What am I trying to do in this problem? Too often a student glances at a problem and starts trying to solve it without first being sure what the question is.
- What is the best way to solve the problem? Ask yourself what process you should use—addition, subtraction, multiplication, or division. If you are dealing with fractions or algebraic equations, what special steps must you keep in mind?

The best way for me would be to use a calculator, but my teacher won't let us.

There's a time and a place for calculators, but not until you have a good foundation in math.

I still don't see why I can't use my calculator.

Suppose your calculator has a bad battery and it says that 6 times 12 is 154. How will you know if that answer is right or wrong?

Well, if the calculator doesn't have some indicator to tell me the battery is low, I guess I wouldn't know.

Before you can rely on a calculator, you must learn how to estimate the correct answer to a problem.

Here's another question you must ask yourself:

- What is a reasonable answer? For example, if you are adding 89534 to 87567, you can look at the two numbers and know that your answer is going to have at least six places in it. Since you know that 8 and 8 add up to 16, there has to be at least one more number in your answer than either of the two numbers you are adding together. Jot that estimate (160000) down next to where you will write your answer. If you come out with the answer 17091, you'll know right away that answer is wrong. It is one figure less than the two numbers with which you started.

You make estimating sound easy, but I think someone has to be good in math to get a pretty decent estimate.
The more math problems you estimate and then work out, the better and more at ease you will be with estimating. Do you know how the Audubon Society teaches people to estimate the number of birds in a flock?

Nope. Can't say that I do!
They have a person grab a handful of beans, throw them on the table, and guess how many beans there are. Then the person counts the beans to see how close their answer was. If they do this enough times, they learn by practice to make very accurate guesses, whether what they are estimating is beans

or birds. The point of this story is that as you practice your math, you become more and more able to judge what the answer should be before you even start to work the problem.

I still don't think estimating will ever be very useful for me.
Pretend someone from another planet shows up. He tells you about a baseball game on his planet and says that his team won the game 1902 to 890. What will you say?

I'll say his baseball game must be different from ours. No baseball game on earth runs up scores that high.
From experience you can estimate that a score like that isn't right for the game you play.

I guess so, but someone from another planet talking to me about baseball isn't very likely!
No, it isn't, but you use math to estimate more than you think. If you're at the mall, you estimate if the money you have in your wallet is enough to buy a tape. If you are on a trip with your parents and your dad says that you'll stop for lunch in the next town, 8 miles away, you will probably glance at your watch without thinking and figure about what time you'll get there. Do you ever shop for groceries for your family?

Sure.

Suppose you buy a quart of milk and a dozen eggs and the clerk at the store says, "$14.32, please." What would you say?

I'd say, "No way. Check that total."
Right. You can probably think of lots more examples in which you use estimating every day.

Doing math in school gives you the practice you need to make accurate estimates in many situations, now and throughout your life. Estimate every time you have a problem to do, especially if you are doing word problems, because they are most like situations in real life in which you will use math.

Word problems are the hardest for me to do.
Sure they are, for you and for most everyone. You are trying to do two things at once—sort of like patting your stomach with one hand and rubbing the top of your head with the other hand. So separate the two parts: (1) understanding what you're being asked, and (2) doing the math.

- First, use language skills to understand the problem. Don't write down numbers without paying attention to the words that help you grasp what you are looking for. Forget the math and forget how you will solve the problem. Look for the main question you are being asked.

Is the main question the last part of the problem, where they tell you what they want you to find?

Usually, but often rewording can help you better understand what you are looking for in solving the problem. What are you being asked to find in this problem? "The train leaves New York at five o'clock. It travels at 60 miles an hour. Washington D.C. is 225 miles away. How far from Washington will the train be at 6:30?"

I'm being asked how far from Washington the train will be at 6:30.
Reword that to ask it another way, a way that will make the question clearer than giving the time on the clock when the train arrives.

I guess I'm supposed to find how far the train goes in one and one-half hours.
Right. When you decide what the main question is, jot it down so you won't forget. Then go on to the next part.

- Second, use math skills to solve the problem. You must decide what figures you need and what process you will use. Only then can you actually do the calculations involved.

What do you mean when you say I have to decide what figures I need?
Sometimes the writers of word problems give what is called *extraneous information.* Extraneous information is a fancy way of saying that they give you extra facts because they want you to decide what numbers are important in solving the problem and what aren't needed. In the above problem, if you had been told that Baltimore is thirty-five miles north of Washington, that would have been extraneous information because the number thirty-five isn't useful in finding the answer that is asked for.

Throwing in extra numbers seems like a pretty sneaky thing to do.
Maybe, but having you choose the numbers you need helps prepare you for real-life math situations. For example, to decide if you have the money to buy a tape advertised as having a $2.00 mail-in-rebate, you must know the cost of the tape and the sales tax. Forget the $2.00. That is extraneous information at the time you buy the tape.

After I decide what numbers I need, I guess I have to figure out what to do with them.
Yes. After you decide which numbers you need, choose the process you should use to answer the question; that is, if you must add, subtract, multiply, or divide.

Remember to jot down your estimate of the final answer. Then do the calculations and compare your answer with the estimate. If they are too far apart, first check your estimate. Then check your math work to be sure you didn't forget something simple or use the wrong process.

If you find out in class that your answer is wrong, write down the correct answer and rework the problem when you have time. Ask for help if you need it, but don't give up until you see both how the correct answer was arrived at and why.

That's not easy for me! I'm so messy that I can't figure out what I did the first time.

Turn your paper sideways and use the lines to help you keep your columns straight. Write only one number between each pair of lines like this:

		8	7	5	
		x	3	2	
	1	7	5	0	
2	6	2	5		
2	8,	0	0	0	

If you don't want to do that, buy some graph paper with large squares and write one number in each square like this:

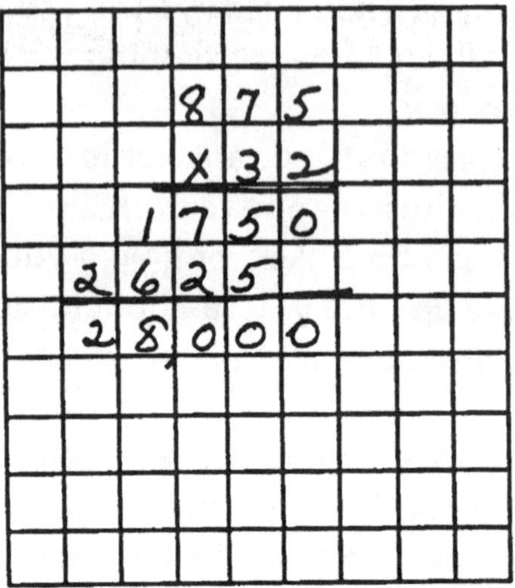

I still don't think I'll ever like math.

You may not like studying math, but learn to love the idea of math. The Bible tells you that even the hairs of your head are numbered. As you go further in math and science you will find that all of nature is ordered according to God's laws and that mathematics helps us understand more about the world we live in. Grammar and spelling are different from one country to another, but everywhere in God's world the laws of numbers are the same. If you are in Japan or in Egypt, one and one still make two. You'll find that to fully appreciate God's natural world or to further God's work, you need to understand that math is basic to everything we do and see.

READING BETTER AND FASTER

Even though math is an important skill to master, much of what you learn in school is learned by reading. You may listen to the teacher and see tapes and demonstrations, but reading is still the main way you master important information and explore new worlds, both real and imaginary. As each school year goes by, you will probably be expected to do more and more reading.

I'm finding that out. I've got a ton of stuff to read by Monday. A novel for a book report in English and two chapters for social studies. For science I even have to read the dictionary—you know, look up the meanings of a bunch of words. I need more time.

Time isn't the real problem. Your real problem is how. How fast you get your work done depends a great deal on how you read.

I don't think I can get everything read by Monday no matter how I go about it.
Maybe you won't get it all done as well as you could have if you had started earlier. But you can do just fine if you really want to. A little prayer to God asking for help to do your best can give you the confidence you need. God will help you do your work, but only if you help yourself.

Look at it this way. If we were to offer you five hundred dollars to get the work done by Monday, could you do it?

Are you kidding! For that I could read two novels by Monday . . . .

Oh! I see what you mean. If I'm willing to work for something, God will help me find a way to do it.
Right. Now let us help you learn some ways to get those assignments done.

When you think about how you read, first consider your speed. Reading speed plays a major part in the way you read.

I think I'm a pretty slow reader.
Ask your teacher to give you a speed-reading test. Or have a friend or parent time you for one minute while you read. Pick material that you know something about and that is not hard reading. A book or magazine you enjoy or a pamphlet from last week's Sunday school class would be good to use. After you finish reading for one minute, test your

understanding; can you tell yourself or someone else what was in the paragraph(s)? Then, to get the number of words per minute (wpm) you read, count the number of words you read. Check your speed several times as you read about several different topics to get a true picture of your average reading speed.

That sounds easy. I think I'll do it.

Knowing your reading rate, however, won't help you finish those assignments unless you push yourself to read faster. For the next week, concentrate on reading as fast as you can while still making sense of what you read. You might want to use the fingertips of one hand or a 3" x 5" card held lengthwise to guide your eyes down the page rapidly. Don't try to read every word. Just get the main ideas. Then take another timed test. Keep pushing, even if you miss a little of what you're reading. To be sure you remember to push yourself to read faster, check your reading speed once a week for several weeks.

If I take a reading test today, will that help me get everything read by Monday?

Not really. Changing reading habits takes a few weeks, but the sooner you start, the sooner you'll pick up speed.

Won't I miss important things if I try to read fast?

Reading is like driving a car. There are times to drive fast, on an interstate, for instance. There are times to drive slowly, like past a school. Reading is the same; there are times to read fast and times to read slowly.

You need flexible reading rates. Before you begin to read, think about why you are reading, and adjust your reading speed with that purpose in mind. As an example, let's use that book report for English class. What's the topic of your report?

A one-page discussion of the main character. Then your purpose in reading is to collect information about the main character. Since you're reading for a book report and you won't be tested on details of the novel, you should read most of the book fairly quickly. To read quickly:

- Pay close attention only to parts of the book that are important for your purpose (in this case, anything to do with the main character).
- Skip information that's not important (in your case, descriptions of scenery or other characters).
- Make notes as you go along and write down the page numbers where you find ideas and facts you'll need later.

But skipping material in the book seems like cheating.

No, it is smart reading to find the information you need. Reading quickly over the information you don't need to locate the important information you do need is called *skimming*. You read fast with a special purpose in mind.

Skimming is what a lawyer does in reviewing cases and doctors do in locating material about drugs and diseases and what your teacher does when finding material needed for a lesson plan. Everyone has to skim to get through the vast amount of material that passes in front of our eyes every day.

Let's say you need to look up something in the Book of Timothy, but you have forgotten just where in the books of the Bible to find Timothy. Look at a list of the books of the Bible, put your brain on automatic pilot, and let your eyes go as fast as they can down the list looking for long words beginning with T. When you get into the New Testament the word TIMOTHY will pop out at you between Thessalonians and Titus.

Just like using the phone book! Now I understand why I need fast reading and why fast reading is okay sometimes. Is there any time slow reading is best?

The last time you put a model together, did you read the instructions very, very slowly?

For sure. Several times. You have to read that way to figure out what they want you to do to make it turn out right.
Exactly. So when your purpose for reading is to follow directions, read slowly and pay attention to each and every detail.

Do you know what my sister did when she made her first cake? She did it in a hurry and read "tablespoon" instead of "teaspoon" and put a tablespoon of salt in it! We had to toss the cake in the garbage.
That's a super example. The importance of slowly reading directions holds true no matter whether the instructions are for baking a cake, doing a science experiment, or taking a test. Read slowly, then go back at least once and check to be sure you have it absolutely right. In chemistry class, read lab instructions three times; the life you save could be your own!

I bet you're going to say that I have to read my textbooks slowly too.
You're almost right. Study-type reading is usually done a little faster than reading directions, but only after you've skimmed the chapter quickly. If you have your social studies book with you, we'll show you what we mean.

Yeah, here it is.
Open it to one of the chapters you've been assigned and let's take a look.

Chapter 4, right here . . . .

The first step in studying a chapter is to preview. A preview of a chapter is like the preview of a movie or TV show. It gives you an idea what's going to be in it.

You're in luck. This textbook starts off with a paragraph that gives you an overview of what the chapter will cover. If there is an overview paragraph, always read it carefully. Then spend some time glancing though the entire chapter. A careful reading of the overview paragraph and quickly skimming through the whole chapter will give you a good idea what the chapter is about.

As you skim you also want to notice information that seems to be especially important. Check out the bold, dark print and captions under the pictures, graphs, and charts.

Finally, read the last paragraph or summary and the questions at the end of the chapter. The questions tell you what information the author thinks you should remember from the chapter. Previewing the chapter by using this process is an important part of studying.

That seems like an awful lot of work. I'll never finish if I do everything twice.

But don't you already have to go back and read stuff twice because you didn't get it the first time?

That's true.

If you preview first, you'll find that reading the

chapter is easier and goes faster than the way you do it now.

I guess you're right. What were those steps again for previewing?
Here they are:

- Read the overview of the chapter carefully.
- Skim through the entire chapter.
- Read carefully the captions under pictures, graphs, and charts and what is stated in **bold, dark print.**
- Read the chapter summary and the questions at the end of the chapter.

Then I go back and read the whole chapter?
Yes. As you read, keep in mind that not all words are created equal. Certain words give important information. Watch for those key words that you first came across when you previewed the chapter. They will often be found in headings or subheadings and if they are in *italicized* type or **boldfaced** print you can be certain they are extra-important words. When you see those words, slow down and be sure you understand what they mean and the way they are used.

My teacher said that if we ask ourselves questions as we read, it will help us learn the material. How can I do that?
Turn headings or subheadings into questions. If the heading is "Joseph's Prophetic Dreams," how could you turn that into a question?

I guess, "What did Joseph's dreams say was going to happen?"

Yes. Then read to find what the dreams were about and what happened to make people understand they were prophetic dreams.

Fiction (novels and short stories writers make up) don't have headings and subheads as most textbooks in science and social studies do. The easiest way to check your understanding of fiction is to ask yourself every page or so, "Does this make sense to me? What did I just read?" Then mentally retell what happened. If you can't retell yourself who the characters are and what they are doing in the story, then you must reread. Sometimes, if the action is hard to grasp, you may need help from a teacher or parent with your rereading.

Even with headings to help, reading a text-book seems a lot harder than reading a novel.

Yes, because you aren't just reading it, you're studying it. Studying means that you're focusing all your attention on learning the information. In most textbooks there is no story line to weave together the facts, details, and ideas. With a story you may want only the general idea of the plot, or action. With a textbook you try to get 100 percent of the ideas. To have such complete understanding, you may have to reread several times.

But isn't reading something over and over a bad habit to have?

Not unless you read that way when you shouldn't. Often you reread because you're thinking about something else. When something is on your mind, write it down or do something about it. If you still have trouble, reading out loud may help you concentrate.

Another reason for rereading is that a book is too hard for you. No matter how thoughtfully you select a slow reading rate and how many times you reread, you simply cannot comprehend what the author is saying. Most likely you don't know the words used in the book or you don't have the background to understand the ideas. You often run into books too hard for you when you're doing research for a report. Don't even try to read and understand a book if you glance over several pages and find five or more words that are unfamiliar to you on each page.

But suppose I have to give a report and need the information.

Find a simpler version on the same topic—even a book for little kids. Your friendly librarian can help. The simpler version will give you an easier vocabulary and the background you need. Then you can go back to the harder book for more in-depth information, if you find you still need it.

If you are reading a book with just a few words new to you, be sure you understand all of those new words. *Don't skip over the ones you don't know*. (See, right there, by underlining those words and putting them in italics, we told you that not skipping words you don't know is very important.)

How did you know I skip words I don't know?
Because you aren't the only person who likes to be lazy! We catch ourselves doing that too when we read difficult books.

Here is a sentence. As you read, try to figure out how to pronounce the long word in it and tell us what it means.

"As he walked, he hoped to find some e-lub-i-plas-mous—elubiplasmus." I think that's how to pronounce it, but I really can't tell what it means.
You pronounced it correctly. You broke the word down into syllables, pronounced each one, and then put them all together. That's the first step when you are confronted with a new word. Sometimes when you pronounce a word out loud and you hear yourself saying the word, your brain may kick in and say, "Oh, yeah, I know that word."

Now what else could you do to figure out the meaning if you still didn't know?

Look it up in the dictionary?
Be honest, is that what you would do next?

Probably not. I'd read on a little more to see if I could figure out the meaning.
And that's what most good readers do. Even though parents and teachers love to say, "Go look it up,"

they probably don't do that themselves until they read on to try to get the meaning. Here are the next two sentences. Now can you tell what the new word means?

"But the sandy beach was barren and he knew that he would go hungry tonight. Perhaps tomorrow an elubiplasmus would wash up on shore and he could dine on the fish like a king." Oh, sure. Elubi-whatever is a type of fish.
But if you hadn't been able to figure out the meaning, what would you do next?

I guess now I should say I'd go find a dictionary, but to tell the truth, I'd probably ask someone else.
Why are we not surprised? Sure, most of us hate to get up to go look for a dictionary. That's why we've learned to keep one on our desk. The farther along you go in school, the more you'll need a dictionary near you all the time.

As for asking someone else . . . well, that ought to be your last step. The person you ask may not know the right answer.

In this case, no one could have helped you—not even the dictionary, because we made up the word so we could be sure you didn't know it.

No wonder I never heard of a elubi-what! But at least I figured it out!
You went through all the right steps. Let's review what

they are. Instead of skipping a word you don't know:

- Say the word aloud (quietly if you are near others). Sometimes you realize that you do know the word once you hear it. If you have trouble pronouncing it or it still doesn't mean anything to you, then . . .
- Try to figure out the meaning of the word by the way it is used. Reread several sentences, skip over the word you don't know for a minute, and then read the next few sentences. You may be able to figure it out from context; i.e., from clues given in the rest of the paragraph. If you still can't figure out the word's meaning, then . . .
- Go to an authority. That authority can be a a person, but first try the glossary in the back of your book or your handy dictionary.

Which brings us back to another part of my homework—looking up all those science terms. My teacher said we have to write them in our own words. Why can't we just copy out of the dictionary?
Your teacher knows that if you can say it in your own words you truly understand what the term means.

I won't have to look up some of the words. Degree is one of them. Everyone knows what "degree" means.
What does it mean?

Get real! Like, when the temperature is freezing, it's thirty-two degrees.

"Degree" is one of those words that has many different meanings, depending on how it's used. Degree can mean temperature and probably does for this assignment. But if your English teacher wants you to learn about degrees of comparison and you use the wrong definition, you may not get that degree at the end of high school!

Don't take learning new words lightly. Usually a teacher gives you words to learn because those words are going to be in the next lesson. If you know them you will be able to better understand the new material coming up. When you read the material with those words in it, it will make better sense and you won't have to skip those words or stop to figure out what they mean.

So can I use some special ways to help me look up the words?

You certainly can. Skim the pages, glancing at guide words at the top, until you find the page you want. Then skim the page to find the word you want. Then check the definitions to find the specific definition that makes sense for the subject you're studying. Read that definition slowly—maybe out loud.

Looking words up is sure no fun, but I guess I see why teachers want us to do it. Reading will NEVER be easy for me, not even with words I know.

Reading is like any skill. The more reading you do, the better you'll be at it. So it is important that you keep reading—just reading and reading and reading will improve your skill in it.

I don't think that's always true. There's a boy in my class who can hardly read anything. He always reads just one word at a time. He keeps trying, but he never gets any better.
Sounds like your friend has a learning disability. He needs special reading help—not because he isn't bright or isn't trying. His brain simply works differently. Be sure to tell him he can learn to read if he gets reading help from a special kind of teacher. If he can't get that help at school, tell him to check out the resources we list in the back of this book.

Let's see if I've got everything we've talked about straight. I need to look at what I'm going to read and decide how fast or slow to read it—slow for details and fast for general stuff. I should read as fast as I can, but still understand what I read. And before I read a chapter in a textbook, I should look for the words and pictures that will help me make sense of what the chapter is about.
And don't forget to concentrate on what you're reading and to work on increasing your vocabulary. When you get better at reading, you'll find that your writing will improve too. We'll see how that works next time.

THE ABCs OF WRITING

Lots of people have trouble putting their thoughts and ideas on paper. And yet if scholars of many years ago had not written down what they had seen and heard and studied, we would not have the Holy Bible.

I'm glad they did, but writing is the hardest part of school for me. I hate it when the teacher assigns us a paper—or even a paragraph.
Why do you dislike writing so much?

Writing takes a lot of time and it's boring. Then the teacher hands back my paper with marks all over it.
Writing isn't so bad if you know how to do it the way it's done by people who write books and articles for

a living. Advanced writers spell correctly, use good grammar, and write fast but effectively. So they use a system—steps they go through—that help them get the most from their writing time. Our writing system, called the ABCs, is based on the steps that published writers use. There are six steps:

- Step #1: A is for Assemble.
- Step #2: B is for Begin.
- Step #3: C is for Create.
- Step #4: D is for Dawdle; don't do anything.
- Step #5: E is for Expose the errors.
- Step #6: F is for Fix.

If you follow our ABCs, you can write more easily and be a better writer; hopefully, the teacher will make fewer marks on your paper. (We won't talk about writing short stories here, but the general ideas and tips will help you do any kinds of writing a teacher may assign.)

Any way is better than the way I'm doing it now!

All right. Let's take it a step at a time.

Step #1: A stands for *Assemble.* No matter what your writing assignment is, whether a sentence, a paragraph, or a longer paper, first you have to choose a topic you're interested in and gather the information you need.

My English teacher usually tells us what to write about, but even if she doesn't, all the topics I think of sound boring.

If you think hard, you can find *something* interesting

about almost any topic. God has made a wonderful world, and it isn't a boring one. Only you can make it seem that way. If the teacher gives you a topic, open your eyes, ask questions, and talk to people to get ideas you can use.

When you need to find your own topic, think about hobbies you enjoy, TV shows you like, trips you've taken, books you've read, things you feel strongly about, walks you've taken in the woods. Whether the topic is the teacher's or your own, if you let yourself be bored, your writing is going to sound even more boring than you feel.

After you settle on a topic, it's time for Step #2. The B is for *Begin*. You begin to pull your thoughts together by organizing them in your mind and by jotting them down on paper.

I guess you mean make an outline. My teacher says to do an outline before we write our paper, but how can I write one until AFTER I write my paper? I may change things all around.

An outline gives you a framework so you can write about your topic in a logical order. Just like going on a trip—you look over a map and plan to take certain roads. Later you may make some changes, but you start off with an idea where you're going and how you're going to get there.

I guess that makes sense, but I still hate to be bothered with putting all those Roman numbers and letters exactly where they should be. If your teacher will let you, try another kind of outline.

You might just write down a list of the main points you'll want to make. Don't bother numbering them.

Here's an even better way. Look at the diagram below. It's called a web because it looks something like a spider's web. To use the web, jot down your topic in the center and in the boxes around it write the points you'll make. When you write, you will connect these ideas and weave them together into a whole. You can use a web to organize the sentences in a paragraph or to organize the parts of a longer paper. After you finish your web, if the teacher requires it, you can convert it into a traditional outline.

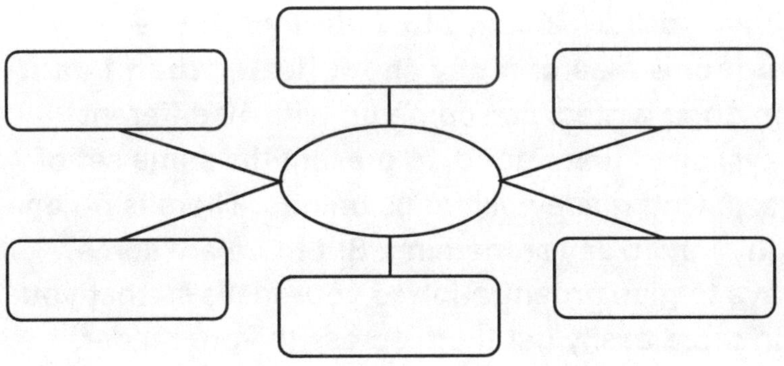

Here is the same web filled in:

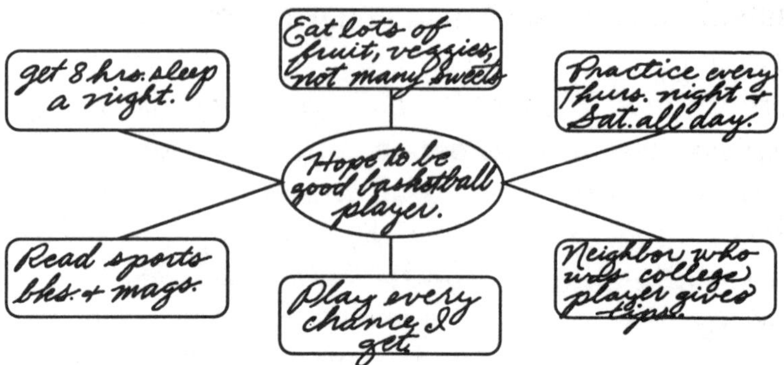

I think I can deal with that kind of outline. What's the next step?

The C in Step #3 stands for *Create*. Don't try to WRITE THE PAPER. The very idea can make your brain go blank. Just jot down thoughts as quickly as they pop into your head. Don't expect your paper to be perfect at this step. Go from point to point on your list, web, or outline and write down everything you can think of—even if some of your ideas sound silly. You can throw something out later.

I have lots of ideas, but I always figure someone else can say them better than I can.

Ten good writers can come up with 10 different ways, all of them good, to present the same set of ideas. God made each of us unique. There is no one right way to say something. But there are some ways to give organization to your ideas so that you can more easily get them across to your reader.

One way is by using number words, such as "the

first step," "my final point," etc. Another way is to go from the general to the specific by making a broad statement and then explaining it. For example, if you said that Jesus' resurrection changed mankind forever, then you would give details and facts to explain your statement.

Giving details and facts is a lot harder than you make it sound. Last week my teacher swapped our papers around. The one I had to read was deadly dull. We were supposed to use 200 words to tell something scary that happened to us, but nothing happened in this girl's paper. She just talked about a big blue lake with tall green pine trees and hundreds of dark clouds like big black balls of fluffy dirty cotton and on and on.

Hopefully, the girl who wrote that paper will learn that writing with too many descriptive words is boring. It sounds as if she used adjectives and adverbs mostly to pad the word count.

Published writers know that active verbs are the most important part of speech. Nouns are the second most important. Vivid verbs and nouns help you be exact, to be *specific*. For example, instead of saying, "He ate fast," say, "He gobbled his pizza." Choose verbs and nouns that say exactly what you mean when you give details.

I always get hung up on writing a beginning.

Just start writing. Trust that later on, as you write, a way to begin will pop in your head. First, put everything you can think to say about your topic onto paper. Then go back later and write your beginning and your ending.

Finding the perfect way to open your paper is a waste of time; don't get so hung up on writing a beginning that writer's block keeps you from moving your pencil onto your paper.

How should I begin my paper when I do write it?
The beginning of a paper introduces the topic to your reader. It should tell the reader what you're going to talk about. Here are some examples:

- If you are describing someone, explain first the point you want to make about him or her.
- If you are writing an essay, clearly state the point you want to make.
- If you are writing a review of a book, identify the title and author and theme (or general nature) of the book.

How about the ending?
The ending is usually simply stating again your introduction in slightly different words. It should wrap everything together. Don't try to be too cute or clever with the ending unless it is an article or story that is supposed to be funny. You can spoil a good paragraph or report that way.

Let's suppose I've written everything I can think of, even a beginning and an ending. What else is left to do?

Nothing! And EVERYTHING! The D of Step #4 of the ABC system stands for *Dawdle; don't do anything.* Let your paper sit while you do something else. You have worked so hard on what you wrote that you need to get away from it for a while. Remember, however, that you have to allow time for this step. You can't let it sit if you finish writing at midnight on a paper that's due the next day. Don't tell yourself that this step isn't important. It is, because it leads to step #5.

Step #5 must be to read back over what I wrote.
Yes, Step #5 is E for *Expose those errors.* After a day or more has passed, take a fresh look at what you wrote. Very few people, including published authors, write perfectly the first time. Check your paper for what are called the *conventions* of writing.

That's a funny word to use. I thought *conventions* were meetings where people from all over, like members of a certain religion, got together to discuss things.
That is one use of the word. In this case, the word means "an accepted way of doing something." Read what you wrote through from beginning to end to check for those conventions, or accepted ways for spelling, grammar, and punctuation. These three may not sound exciting, but paying attention to them can make writing easy to read and understand. The best ideas in the world aren't readable unless you follow the conventions of writing.

Here's a quick checklist to help when you proofread.

read Is your handwriting or typing easy to read and neat, with mistakes carefully corrected?
—> Did you indent each paragraph?
C Did you use capitals with care?
spell Did you spell with care?
, Did you use commas in the right places?
" " If you quoted, did you use quote marks?
. ? ! Did you use the right mark at the end of each sentence?

Remember: **read —> C spell, "."**

These symbols will remind you of the proofreading steps to take before handing in a paper, whether it is a sentence, a report, or an essay-type test. In fact, write on the inside cover of your notebook or somewhere where you can turn to it easily:

read —> C spell, "."

I have trouble spelling. I just don't notice that a word isn't spelled right.

Here are some things you can do if spelling is an area in which you have trouble:

- Use a dictionary to check the spelling of a word if you are not absolutely sure of its spelling. Keep a list in a small memo book or the back of your notebook of commonly used words that you often misspell.
- Buy an electronic speller or ask for one as a Christmas or birthday gift. With an electronic speller you type the word in incorrectly and the

machine will show you how to spell it correctly. There is also a special paperback dictionary that doesn't cost much. It tells you a correct spelling when you look up the wrong one.

- Finally, ask a friend or family member to mark incorrectly spelled words with a light checkmark over a word.

But you aren't done with Step 5. *Expose the errors* also means a special reading to check the *content* of your paper. Did you say what you meant to say?

What do I look for when I read for content? Check if you listed all the important points. Note if the beginning and ending sound right. Do they tell the reader what the paper is going to be about/what it was about? Close your eyes and try to visualize in your mind what you wrote. Find one thing you truly like about what you wrote. Find one thing you think you should change. If it were not your writing, how would you feel about it? What and how could you rewrite to make it more interesting?

When I read over something it always seems okay to me. But then the teacher finds a lot of stuff wrong and draws arrows all over my paper. Perhaps you are not yet at the stage in writing when you can judge for yourself what you have written. Work toward separating *what* you have said from *how* you have said it. What you say may not be what you mean or may not be the *best* way to say it.

You can also ask someone else to read your paper. Trade papers with a classmate and react to each other's writing. Tell each other what you like best about the other paper. When either of you sees something you think should be changed, don't rewrite for the other person—just make a pencil check in the margin where they need to rework what was said.

Then always *read what you have rewritten* ***aloud.*** A sentence may look great on paper, but if it sounds dumb when you read it out loud, that's how it will strike the reader, for sure.

Now you're ready for the last step, #6.

F must have something to do with correcting my mistakes, right?

Exactly right. Step # 6, F is for *Fix.* Since Step #5, Expose the errors, means catching mistakes in wording plus mistakes in the conventions of English (spelling, grammar, and mechanics), fixing mistakes means making the changes needed.

Since these changes may involve moving around sentences or whole paragraphs, cutting parts out, and saying some things in ways that are different and easier to understand, allow time for rewriting. Many published writers rewrite their materials eight or ten or more times, so plan on doing at least one or two rewrites on every paper. If it is an important paper that carries a major grade, you may need to rewrite it several times.

Wow! Writing is a lot of work!

It certainly is, but, like any other skill, you can become better the more writing you do. Here are the ABCs again, so you can be sure you got them all:

- Step #1: A is for Assemble
- Step #2: B is for Begin
- Step #3: C is for Create
- Step #4: D is for Dawdle; don't do anything
- Step #5: E is for Expose the errors
- Step #6: F is for Fix

Whether you are using pen, pencil, or computer, use these steps to express your ideas like a professional writer.

My teacher sometimes doesn't want to know only our ideas. She wants us to look up what others have written and make a report. Any special way to help me with that?

Yes, use a card-organizing system to help you do research. Let's talk about how to write that special kind of paper— a report or research paper.

RESEARCHING & REPORTING

Chapter FIVE

Everything we said about writing applies to writing reports or research papers. But we have some extra ideas that will help you organize your material and will make your job of writing a report or research paper easier in the long run. Organizing is a very important part of writing a report. If you look at your Bible, you will see that it is organized according to certain topics. If the various parts of the Bible were scattered all around, you would find it much harder to understand.

What's the difference between writing a report (or research paper) and other kinds of writing? Is it just that reports and research papers are longer?

No, although a research paper is usually longer than

other writing you do in school. The big difference is that a report (or research paper) does not give your ideas, opinion, or point of view. A book report may include your opinion of the book, if the teacher asks for it.

You said when I pick a topic for a short paper, I should pick something I'm really interested in. Is that still okay advice?
Yes, it is. Once you think of an interesting topic, pick some very small part of that broad subject. You might think the broader the topic, the better, but too much information makes a paper hard to organize. For example, let's say you're interested in writing about missionaries. But lots of books have been written about that topic. You should pick one small piece of the general subject of missionaries.

You mean, like "Missionaries in China"?
Narrow the topic even more. You would have enough material for a full paper if you looked only at the work of one special missionary whose life interests you.

Then it's time to begin taking notes.

When I have to take notes from different books and magazines, I have lots of trouble.
That's where the card-file system comes in. Before you rush to the library to find facts and scribble them on cards, you must do some groundwork to make your investigation into the subject easier and more efficient. So first, as soon as you decide on a

topic, ask yourself what you'd like to know about that topic.

How do I do that?

Let's say that you are to write a paper on the topic of deserts of Israel. What are some questions you might ask?

I guess I'd want to know what a desert is and why it doesn't rain . . . and if it's hot in the desert, even at night.

So the questions you'd start with are:

1. What is a desert?
2. Why doesn't it rain in the desert?
3. Is it hot both day and night in the desert?

Write the questions on a single sheet of paper and number them as we did. If you want to use a web, write the topic of your paper in the center and a numbered question on the ends of the threads of the web. These are the questions you'll use to start the research for your paper. You don't have to use all the boxes. Leaving empty spaces gives you a place to add others as you delve into your topic.

Now you are ready to find information that will answer those questions, and perhaps others that come to mind as you read.

Now I go to the library?

For starters, yes. Librarians like to offer help to students, so visit both your school library and your public library. Begin by learning how to use the catalogs, whether they are on cards, computer, or microfiche. The librarian can also direct you to a whole group of specialized reference books and several types of encyclopedias.

My teacher doesn't like us to use encyclopedias.
Most teachers are afraid that if you use an encyclopedia, you will copy straight from it and not do your own research and writing. Copying someone else's writing is a kind of cheating. So sum up information in your own words when you take notes.

Then why did you say to use an encyclopedia?
An encyclopedia is great for giving you an overview of your subject. It will also give you ideas and key words to use in rooting out your topic in other places, such as a computer search if your library is linked to a service for searching data bases. If it does, learn how to request one. Your savings of time and effort may more than offset the small cost.

But don't stop with the library. Consider using unusual sources of information such as interviewing, writing away for information, and asking friends and professionals. If your topic is "Deserts of Israel," you could write to the Embassy of Israel plus talk to a minister who took a trip over there. People you interview can tell you useful information and probably also lead you to new resources you haven't located elsewhere.

Whatever sources you use, start taking notes on cards *as soon as you begin* or you'll forget a lot of the great information you find.

I write *really* large. Can I use loose-leaf paper instead of cards?

The reason for using cards is that you want to be able to shuffle them around later on. Some students do use loose-leaf paper, but because cards are sturdier, they're easier to handle. Here's what is super-important: Put *only one idea* on each card or sheet.

That seems like a big waste of paper no matter how you do it.

The time you'll save when you begin to write far outweighs using extra cards or paper. We'll explain later. For now, look at this sample:

> Baedeker's Israel, p. 17 (3.)
>
> In southern Israel in winter (Nov.-Mar.), days are warm, nights cool, but way above freezing.

At the top left side of your card, summarize all information about your source. That would be the book or magazine and page number.

If you're going to do a bibliography later, you'll also need the full name of the author and title, city where published, and the publisher. Write out complete information for a bibliography only once, on a separate card or sheet of paper.

At the top right-hand side of your card, put down the number of the question you're answering. For example, the second question you asked was why it doesn't rain in the desert, so you'd write the number 2, on the cards that answer that question.

When you're ready to organize your paper, you'll stack the cards by number, based on the questions you wrote down when you first began your paper. That means all the #2 cards about "why the desert doesn't get rain" are together.

If I interview someone, do I take notes on what they say too?

Yes. Sum up what they said as you would summarize what you read.

If you want to use someone's exact words, put quotation marks around what they said. Use quote marks whether you use the exact words of your next-door neighbor or a sentence from a book. Quote marks show the reader that someone else deserves credit for those words. Also give the person's name, to show who made the statement.

Suppose I didn't find any information to answer one of the questions?

You can return to the library to get more information, or you may decide after all your reading that the question doesn't seem particularly important. If it isn't important, toss it.

I like that! What's next?

Organize the cards within each number. This step is important—it takes the place of a long, fancy outline. If you have three cards giving information on why it doesn't rain in the desert, decide which one should come first, second, and third. Stack them in that order.

When you read over the cards you may decide to move the numbers around to a different order. For example, you may move the entire set of #3 cards ahead of the #2 cards. That's okay. You want the ideas to flow smoothly. Once you have the cards in the order that makes sense to you, number all the cards in order in a new color ink.

Why renumber them? That seems like an extra step!

As you work with them, they may get out of order. You may also drop them or your little brother may tease you by tossing them in the air. No matter if any of those things happens; you can put them all together again in the right order quickly.

Your paper is now organized and the writing is a breeze. Just go from card to card, turning what's on each card into complete sentences. Connect them with transition words like *next, on the other hand,* and *at the same time.*

If it's a long paper, I can't get it all written at one time. The next evening getting back into writing is even harder than getting started the first time.

If you know the paper will take more than one writing session, don't suddenly quit writing. Stop in the middle of an interesting point. Mark on your note card where you are stopping so you can pick up the next evening.

Since we speak faster than we write or type, you might want to talk the first draft of your report into a tape recorder. You could also ask someone in the family to talk over your report with you while you tape your conversation. Telling someone can often spark new ideas that you alone might never have thought of.

My dad is always asking what I did in school today. Maybe I can "tell" my paper to him. Let me be sure I have the steps straight:

- **First, I pick my topic and ask myself questions about my topic.**
- **Then I find information that answers those questions and put that information on note cards.**
- **Third, I organize my note cards in the order I want to write the report and renumber them with a different color ink.**

- **Next, I go from card to card and write my paper.**

Right?
Exactly right. Then the DEF of the ABC system is the same for finishing your report or research paper as it is for a shorter paper. Do you remember those steps?

I think so:
- **I don't touch my paper for a few days.**
- **I look back over it to find problems with what I said, and I also check for errors in spelling, grammar, and punctuation.**
- **I fix my errors before I turn my paper in.**

Well said! If you follow those steps you'll turn in a great-looking paper that you can be proud you wrote.

Now if you could just help me do better in my other classes.
I think we can do that with the secrets of active listening!

LISTENING & TAKING NOTES

Listening is a problem many students have. God gave us these wonderfully strange things called ears. If you are lucky enough to have a working pair, God expects you to listen not only to His word, but to all the important things your parents and teachers want you to learn.

My hearing is fine. I had it tested the other day. There's a lot more to being a good listener than being able to hear. Let's look at what happens when you listen. First, there must be a sender who makes some sounds. Then there must be a receiver. That's you! A tape recorder "hears" sounds, but it cannot actively listen, as a human can. Active listening is a complex skill that requires you to do two things: *concentrate* and *understand*. Being a good active listener is partly an ability God gives you when you're born and partly a skill you can learn. Since it is partly learned, you can increase how well you do it.

I have trouble concentrating for more than about ten or fifteen minutes max. Then my mind wanders off and I'm thinking about a dozen other things.

Some teachers call ten or fifteen minutes the "TV listening time." Most people who have grown up with TV are used to listening for only that long and then breaking for a commercial.

That's me! Maybe teachers should use commercials.

Lots of good teachers do vary their teaching every little while. But the main job is up to you. You have to want to listen. Unless you're convinced that YOU want to do something, you aren't going to do it very well. That means you must be prepared to give your full attention to the teacher when you go to class.

Try to sit near the front if you have serious trouble staying on task. It's much easier to pay attention if you aren't watching other people. Also,
if you sit up front teachers are more likely to notice any problems you have. They get signals from you that they are talking too fast or that they have made a confusing point.

Most days I do okay, but other days my mind keeps drifting away.

Then try this: When your mind wanders, make a check mark in a corner of your notes and then force yourself to go back to listening. Every time your mind wanders, make another check. Moving to make checks will help you become aware how often your mind wanders and you will begin to stay on task.

If your mind keeps going back to a problem that's really troubling you, write that problem down on a piece of paper. Say a quick little prayer, asking God to help you solve that problem. Then jot down a specific time when you'll focus on solving what is bothering you. You can go back to listening, knowing that you and God will work on it when the time is right.

Sometimes a teacher will say something that gets me upset. I get offtrack thinking about it. Suddenly I come to and realize I don't even know what she's moved on to talk about.
When you realize that something has upset you, dropping that topic and not thinking about it is very hard. Suppose you are worrying about your parents splitting up, and the teacher just happens to mention the divorce rate in talking about something else. When that happens, you may get so upset thinking about your parents that you forget everything else. Again, jot down a note; tell God you need some help. Then try to forget it and get back on task. Later you can talk with the teacher. Explain what happened and ask for some catch-up help. Most teachers will truly understand.

How about asking a question? Sometimes I do that to help me stay interested.

That's fine. But if the teacher doesn't let you interrupt, write a question in your notes that you would ask if you could. It will still help you focus your mind on the topic.

What if I find I've just drifted off for no particular reason and missed the last few sentences?

Then admit to drifting off. Hold up your hand and say, "I'm sorry, I missed that point. Would you repeat that again please?" That will give you a fresh start. You can't do that very often, but most teachers don't mind it once in a while. They know you're trying.

I have a real hard time trying to concentrate in any class that comes after lunch. I'm so sleepy that I have to struggle to stay awake—much less take notes and understand what the teacher's talking about.

First, be sure you aren't watching TV too late. God gave us the power to sleep and rest our bodies, and He expects us to use that to keep our bodies healthy.

If you're getting enough sleep, talk to the teacher about that class. If you feel sleepy, probably everyone else does too. Ask the teacher to open a window or to let everyone get up and stretch a couple of times.

What you eat for lunch may also affect you. Lots of candy and other sweets can make it more difficult for you to stay alert. Ask your librarian for a good nutrition book, or talk to your school nurse to find out what foods would help you stay alert and what foods are more likely to send you nodding.

Everyone has a downtime. Be aware of when yours is and be very sure you keep up with the homework in the class you have then. Knowing what the teacher is talking about will help you understand, even when you are not at peak concentrating form. Although concentrating is important, understanding what you hear is the second important part of active listening.

Say some more about understanding . . . Do you just mean knowing the words the teacher uses? No. Understanding in this case means not only making sense of the words the teacher uses, but also knowing what the teacher considers important. (And of course what the teacher considers important will usually be on the test!)

How do I know what's important? Teachers sometimes talk on and on and I don't know what to pay attention to.

Listen for phrases like:

- "The most important . . . ."
- "The first reason . . . ."
- "It is significant that . . . ."

Listen for words that key you to an understanding of what the teacher's focus is. Be especially alert when a teacher says:

- "I want you to remember . . . ."
- "This will be on the test."

Star those notes so they get top priority when you study.

"Listen" to the teacher's body language as well. Often the teacher's body language lets you know what that teacher thinks is important. For instance, your math teacher may tap on the board with his finger.

Watch the teacher's face. A good place to look is at the teacher's forehead, right between the eyes. Looking there will help you see every facial expression, every movement of the teacher. Each teacher has his or her own body language.

Tell me how I can take notes better. I take too many, I guess, because after a while my hand gets tired and I quit.

The easiest way to cut down the number of classroom notes you take is to do all homework before you go to class. If what the teacher talks about is in the book, merely write down a few words to remind you. If the teacher is giving you new information, then take fuller notes.

A couple of my friends write so slowly that they don't even try to take notes if the person is talking fast.

Tell them not to write down every word. Develop your own shorthand. Most words like *a* or *and* or *the* can be skipped without losing meaning. Also, use capital letters for a word that is repeated. If the lecture is about the Philistines, write the word once. After that use only the letter P as an abbreviation. Be sure to write at the top of the page what the P stands for. If you were taking notes on both Philistines and Pharisees today, you might not remember which you meant a month from now at test time.

What's the best form for taking notes?

There is no best form, despite what you may have heard. You'll have to develop your own form—or forms, to be more accurate. People have different learning styles, different studying styles, and different needs for notes. Some people need a lot more notes than other people do. You also may need to take notes in a different form for science class than you do for social studies.

My teacher told me that the best way is to take notes in outline form.

That's okay if the speaker is orderly and talks in an outline form—but that rarely happens. Usually teachers start off with an outline, but because of questions, they go off into other ideas, not always in an orderly way. When that happens, you have to take notes the best you can.

An outline can also be a problem if you get hung up on whether your next item is a Roman numeral III or the letter B. Look at the end of this book for some common note-taking forms that other people have found useful. Notice that one of the forms looks much like the web we talked about in chapter 3. Using a diagram or drawing helps some students concentrate. The visual picture also helps understanding—both of the pieces of active listening.

Try each type of note taking we show you and adapt the one you like best to your style. Good notes are vital. Without them you cannot expect to make good grades.

A friend of mine has such a hard time trying to listen and take notes at the same time that she misses all the important stuff and then flunks tests. Why does she have so much trouble doing both at the same time?
No one knows, exactly. But we do know that some people have that problem. There are a couple of ways she can be helped. A tape recorder is one idea, but she will have to allow a much longer studying time to replay the whole tape, unless she gets the kind of machine that speeds up the voice

but still keeps the speech clear.

A much better way is for her to work out a deal with you. You take good notes on duplicating paper that doesn't require carbons. You can buy that kind of paper at any office supply store. After class, you give her a copy of the notes. She can then concentrate on learning by listening. Perhaps she can do you a favor, like typing your term paper.

Incidentally, it's good to take notes on noncarbon paper for a friend who is out sick. Always tell the teacher what you are doing and why. Helping a sick friend is a good way of showing Christian care.

That's cool! My friend and I can take turns using that paper. One of us can take notes each week while the other one sits back and relaxes.

Hold it! Most people learn while they take notes. The carbonless paper is an emergency measure for some people and for special situations, not a substitute for your daily work. When it comes time to study for a test, you'll be seeing those notes for the first time if you weren't the one to take them. The physical act of writing helps most people remember the important items come test time.

Do I take notes when I read my textbook the same way I take notes when a teacher talks?

Again, you want to take notes the way that best suits your learning style. Here are some ideas you can try:

- Outline the chapter. The very act of writing may help you learn the material if you are the kind of person who learns best by doing.
- Jot down only a few points that are hard to remember if you can learn just by looking at the book.
- Use a highlighter pen to call attention to special points instead of taking notes if you own the book. Don't highlight everything or the main points won't stand out.
- Photocopy only a single page if you want to write on or mark on a special chart and you don't own the book.
- Use paper clips to mark important pages. Colored clips can mean different things. In a history book, for example, laws could be marked with a blue clip, causes for wars with red, summary of a President's term in office with yellow, and so on.
- Talk about the chapter into a tape recorder and later play your own words back if you learn best by listening rather than looking.

The whole point of making any kind of notes when you read a textbook is to fix the information in your mind and to provide a way for quick review at test time.

And speaking of test taking, let's talk about how to use your notes to study for tests. In the long run, it's those test grades that will make the biggest impact on your report card.

TAKING TESTS

Without a doubt, the words students hate to hear most are, "We are having a test in this class tomorrow."

Boy, you're right. Everyone in class groaned today when my history teacher said that. I've been doing my homework, but I'll still be up all night cramming.

Staying up all night isn't a good idea. You'll be zonked out by testtime. When you take a test you need to eat healthy foods, get a little exercise, and have a good night's sleep. If you've been keeping up with the reading and classwork, what makes you think you'll have to cram?

Well, today my teacher told us what will be on the test. She said we have to know the names of the 13 original states and the first 10

presidents. I'll never get them all in my brain by tomorrow.
Cramming certainly sounds like the answer to that problem, but it won't take all night.

Wait a minute! My parents always say cramming doesn't work.
If by cramming you mean not doing any reading or assignments until the last minute, your parents are right—it won't work. But if by cramming you mean last-minute memorizing of word lists that you'll need just for the test, then it's okay. Cramming is a good way to remember facts, such as dates and names. In other words, it is useful for the kind of information that you probably won't use often and can easily look up when you need it in the future.

What's the best way to cram? Just say the stuff over and over until I think I've got it?
That works, but you can speed up your study time by using tricks to boost your memory. The most common trick is one you've probably already learned. You use the first letter of each word in a list and make up a sentence using those same first letters. As an example, let's think up a sentence that uses the first letter of the first ten presidents in order. Do you happen to have the list handy?

Right here. "Washington, Adams, Jefferson, Madison, Monroe, John Quincy Adams, Jackson, Van Buren, Harrison, and Tyler."
Here's an example of a first-letter trick that would

help you keep the names in the right order. "We ate jam most Mondays. John Q. jumped Van's huge tiger." You could also make up a sentence that has a few of the sounds of the names in it. How about "I washed Adam's jalopy; mad Monroe juggled Jack's very heavy tires"? Research shows that the crazier the words, the better it helps you remember the original list.

Great! If I practice a couple times this afternoon I'm sure I can remember that.
Review again tonight before bed and especially tomorrow morning while you're dressing for school. Research also shows that reviewing several times between now and test time is better than repeating it many times in one session.

And don't forget to go over the names themselves. All the sentences in the world won't jog your memory if you never knew the list to begin with. That's the main problem with memory tricks. You can spend too much time thinking them up and not enough on going over the material itself.

Now all I need is a trick for remembering the colonies.
Visualizing is another kind of trick you could use. Look carefully at a map of the 13 states. Then close your eyes and try to see the map in your mind. As you mentally move your eyes down from Massachusetts to Georgia, focus on each one and its shape. Then say its name.

We traveled through most of the states on the East Coast last year when we went to Florida. I remember a lot about the states we went through.

That's even better. Tie the 13 states to something interesting you remember about each one—maybe a restaurant or something you saw or read. This pulls memories that help you link personal information with new information. Information tied to personal experience is always more easily remembered.

Finally, some people remember better if they can "sing" a list , so they "sing" the word list to some familiar tune like "Row, row, row your boat." It all depends on how your mind works best. But remember, these tricks are good only for short-term memory of word lists.

Why can't I cram anything but word lists?

Cramming is fine for a small amount of information you need to remember for only a day or two. But really learning the ideas and facts you'll need for a long time takes place best when the material is:

- repeated over and over,
- spaced out in time, and,
- tied in with other information that you already know.

When I get ready to study for a test, I start to panic. I know a lot but it all seems to drain out of my brain.

Studying for a test is mostly a matter of attitude. If

you've been doing your homework and going to class, you know the material, but you'll need to refresh your mind.

Start your studying by saying a little prayer asking God to help you concentrate and use your mind to do well. Then mentally picture yourself doing well on the test. Picture the teacher handing back your paper with a great grade on the top.

Don't say things like, "I'll never learn this!" Learning is actually slowed down when you start thinking you'll fail. Instead, say to yourself, "With God's help, I can do this. I know I can."

So how should I start, once I see myself doing well on the test?

Begin by going over bold type in the chapters. Read through your notes. Try summarizing them in your head or writing them down. Most important, think of what questions YOU would ask if you were the teacher. What do YOU think are the main ideas?

If it is a math test, review needed formulas and be sure you know them. Try writing them without looking at the book. Do simple examples of each kind of problem.

If the test is on a novel, you may want to skim a summary of the novel. You can buy summaries of them in paperback. But don't ever think you can use those notes instead of reading the book—that won't work.

I have a friend who wants to study with me. Is that okay?

Studying with a friend works great for some people but not for others. Studying together will work only if both of you are serious about studying and have a positive attitude. If you study with someone who is scared about the exam, that feeling will rub off on you and you won't do as well.

When you work together, don't use the time listening to "just one more cut" on a favorite tape or chattering about all your friends and the party next week. Allow ten minutes at the start for fun and then get to work.

One good way for two people to study together is for each to make up questions and test the other. You can also call off vocabulary lists for English, science, or a foreign language. Remember to compare notes. One of you may have picked up on an important point that the other one missed.

On test day I'm going to hurry to class, and when I get my paper, write as fast as I can before I forget it all.

We understand why you want to "write it as fast as you can," but to make your best grade, don't be in such a rush. Make a rest room stop right before the test. Most teachers won't let you leave the room during the test, and you need to feel as comfortable as you can. Also, if it's allowed, nibble a piece of fruit or some nuts just before you go into class so you'll have some quick energy.

Don't listen to the horror stories of the others or their bragging about what they studied. That can make you lose confidence in yourself. Research shows you'll do your best if you feel just a bit uptight, but not all stressed out.

Have any teachers given you ideas about how to do your best?

Sure. Things like, "Keep your first answer—unless you are absolutely sure it's wrong" and "Take an extra pen or pencil so you don't waste time finding one." Stuff like that.

Those are good ideas, but let's talk about some testing skills that can actually earn you extra points on the test. Just knowing the answers won't always get you your highest grade.

Skill Number One: *Read the directions before trying to write any answers down.*

Why bother with the directions? They usually say the same old thing.

But suppose this time the teacher says to use + and - instead of True and False or to mark your answer with a pencil in the correct square? Lots of teachers want you to use easy-to-score symbols. They may not score a paper incorrectly marked. You *must* take the time to read directions carefully.

Another mistake is not noticing what words are in the directions. Suppose the directions say to "discuss" three reasons. If you pay attention only to the three reasons part, you'll lose points by simply listing them, since discussing means talking about the reasons from various points of view. Directions tell you *exactly* what the teacher wants.

Reading directions can raise questions to ask the teacher before you begin the test. For example, in a math test, ask if you can earn partial credit for estimating the answers if you run out of time. A number of partial points would probably gain you more than would one answer correct to the nearest tenth.

What's the second skill?

Skill Number Two: *Scan the whole test quickly before you begin answering.*

If one question requires several answers, put one check in the margin for each part to be completed. For example, if you're asked to list a major American writer during colonial times and also tell the name of something the person wrote, mark two checks next to that question. Later on, when your mind is befuddled with what you've answered and how much time you have left, you'll remember that question has two parts.

I never thought of making marks to remind me. What can I do about running out of time?

Skill number 3: *Keep track of your time.*

As you read through the test, note the number of points each section is worth so that you can budget your time. If your teacher hasn't indicated point value, ask. Roughly divide your time among the parts, based on how much each will add to your grade. Try to give yourself a few extra minutes to go over the test before you hand it in. Use those few minutes to check for skipped questions or to change answers you know are wrong.

Essay questions are often worth a good bit. If so, allow plenty of time to write a really good paragraph. Keep the ABCs of writing in mind as you answer essay questions. You may want to jot down main points or make a quick web for the answer as soon as you read the question, so you won't forget any facts even if you don't write the complete answer until later.

Essay questions are usually hard for me, so I like to answer them first.

Good point. As you're reading over the test, decide the order in which you'll work on each section. No law says that you have to answer the parts of the test in the order the teacher wrote them. For example, if you are afraid you'll forget your word lists, and you see you'll need them, write them down before you do the other questions. Then you can forget them.

WARNING! It *is* dangerous to skip about if you are using a machine-scored answer sheet. One answer out of place can cause all the rest to be wrong. Machines don't allow for slips of the pencil. So be *sure* that you are marking your answer in the right place. Work straight through the questions. If you aren't sure of one, mark it anyway, but put a check beside it that you can erase later when you go back and think about it some more.

I hate machine-scored tests. Last time I missed some questions because I changed my mind and marked a different answer and

didn't get the first one erased.
On a machine-scored test, allow yourself at least a couple of minutes—even if you don't finish the test—to quickly check every answer, be sure you have fully erased any answer you changed, and notice that you have only one answer per line.

Sometimes I get so hung up on a hard question I don't even have time to answer the ones I know.
Don't ever spend a lot of time struggling with any one answer, even for a question that's worth a lot of points. Go on and come back to it. Then try rephrasing the question in your own words. Once you fully understand the question, you can think about it more clearly. The answer may come to you then.

On a test last week I couldn't remember the answer to an important question and then, *bam,* another question reminded me of the answer to the first one.
That's another reason you shouldn't waste time on any single question. One thought triggers another as you get rolling through the test. Be sure to keep your eyes open for a test question that gives you the answer to another question somewhere else in the test.

On a really long test, stand up and stretch about halfway through the test and, if your teacher allows it, sharpen your pencil or get a drink of water. Standing up and walking about may relax you and help you think of an answer you haven't been able to remember. Be sure that when you take a break, though, that you keep your mind on the test. Don't be distracted by other people or what's going on in the hall outside. Keep focused.

What about guessing?

If you're taking a test that takes points off for guessing, don't. But trust yourself to know most of the answers. Skip only the ones you don't have any idea about.

But what if the teacher doesn't take points off for guessing?

Some people think that guessing is cheating. For example, if the teacher grades on the curve and you use a guessing plan that the other students don't know about, you have an unfair advantage. We suggest you have a class discussion about guessing and decide whether guessing is okay.

I never heard of a guessing plan.

Just plain guessing is as likely to get you no points as it is to get you lots. But using a guessing plan will usually get you a few extra points. On a national standardized, timed test where points aren't subtracted for wrong answers, you can be fairly sure that other students *will* use a guessing plan.

The plan most used is this:

- If you don't have any idea what the answer is, pick false on true/false questions that use words like "always" or "never." Mark as true all the other ones you don't know.

- On multiple-choice questions, choose all b's or all c's if there are 4 choices. If there are five choices pick all c's or all d's.
- On fill-in-the-blanks or completion questions, write an answer if you can think of anything that's even close.

Remember, though, getting points for those questions doesn't mean you knew the answers. After you get the test back, go over the ones you guessed at and learn the right answers. You may need that information later in the year.

I suppose there's no way to guess on short-answer or essay tests, is there?

Not really. We know of one student who got partial credit for a really funny short answer. The teacher said it gave her a laugh. That doesn't happen very often, but it does prove that when you have nothing to lose, you may have points to gain by filling in something.

If you find you can answer all but one essay question, write down a really good question the teacher *might* have asked and answer it. Explain that you studied that question, but not the one the teacher asked. Sometimes a teacher will give some credit because you show you studied. Don't plan on doing that often, though.

You know what I hate? It's when I'm only about half done and some speed demon in the front row turns their paper in. Then I just know I'm going to fail.

Don't even think of trying to compare yourself with others when you're taking a test. If you've done the assignments, read the text, and listened in class, you'll do your best. Don't let yourself fail because of negative thinking. Let go, and let God help you help yourself. Turn that negative nervous energy into positive power. God is on your side.

Hey, maybe I *can* do okay on that test tomorrow. I really have learned everything that's supposed to be on it, except for that stuff I have to cram. Maybe I can do pretty

well. You know, I think I'm going to see some higher grades on my next report card if I try some of the ideas we've been talking about. That's the way to think. Never forget, in God's eyes you are a very important person with a wonderful future ahead. It's up to you to fulfill God's plan by becoming the best you can be. That doesn't mean you have to make all A's. If you really *try* to do the best you can, even though you goof up sometimes, you'll make all A's in God's eyes and that's what counts.

Go in grace and have your finest school year ever.

Resources for students for reading/learning problems:

C.h.A.D.D.
Children with Attention Deficit Disorders
499 N.W. 70th Avenue, Suite 308
Plantation, FL 33317
305/587-3700

International Reading Association
800 Barksdale Raod
P.O. Box 8139
Newark, DE 19714-8139
302/731-1600

Learning Disabilities Association
4156 Library Road
Pittsburgh, PA 15234

Orton Society
Chester Bldg., Suite 382
Baltimore, MD 21286-2044
410/296-0232

Also contact the College of Education of nearby colleges and universities. Many maintain a list of local professionals who are qualified to assess and tutor students with reading/learning difficulties. They may also sponsor clinics to identify and remediate academic problems.

NOTE-TAKING SAMPLES

Listing: A simple listing by letters of the alphabet or numbers separates information, but doesn't show you what at the time seemed important. Putting a star by special facts that are sure to be on a test will help solve that problem.

___/___/9__

1.

2.

3.

4.

Outline: Note taking this way separates the material so you can locate important information to study when test time comes. Information is also condensed and grouped to help you study. Using an outline form takes careful listening on your part, however, if you want to catch main and subheadings. A teacher who is organized in presenting information makes your job easier.

___/___/9__

I. Main idea
   A. Information that explains the main idea
   B. Information that explains the main idea
   C. Information that explains the main idea

II. Main idea
   A. Information that explains the main idea
      1. Example of A.
      2. Example of A.
   B. Information that explains the main idea, etc.

Key words with running notes: Noting key, or important, words in a column to the left helps you study. When you review for a test, simply fold the paper on the dotted line and ask yourself what you remember about the key word. Or cover the key words, look at the notes and identify the important vocabulary that goes with those notes. The notes can be written using a listing format, outline format, or any other style you wish.

Key Words	Notes	___/___/9__

Note–Taking Web: Using a web allows you to go in

all directions with boxes for main ideas and smaller boxes to represent ideas under main ideas—sort of a graphic outline form.

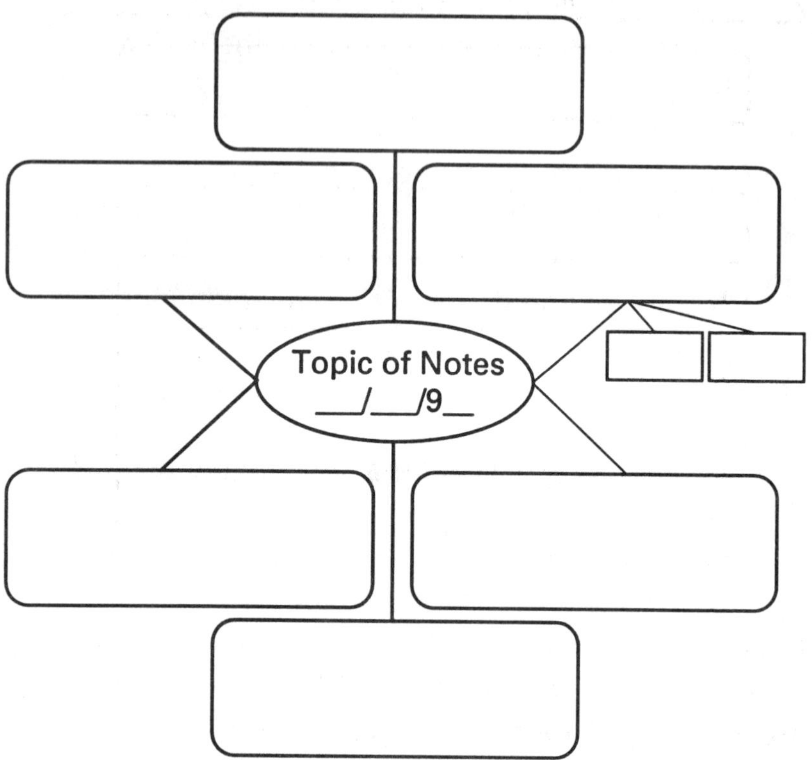

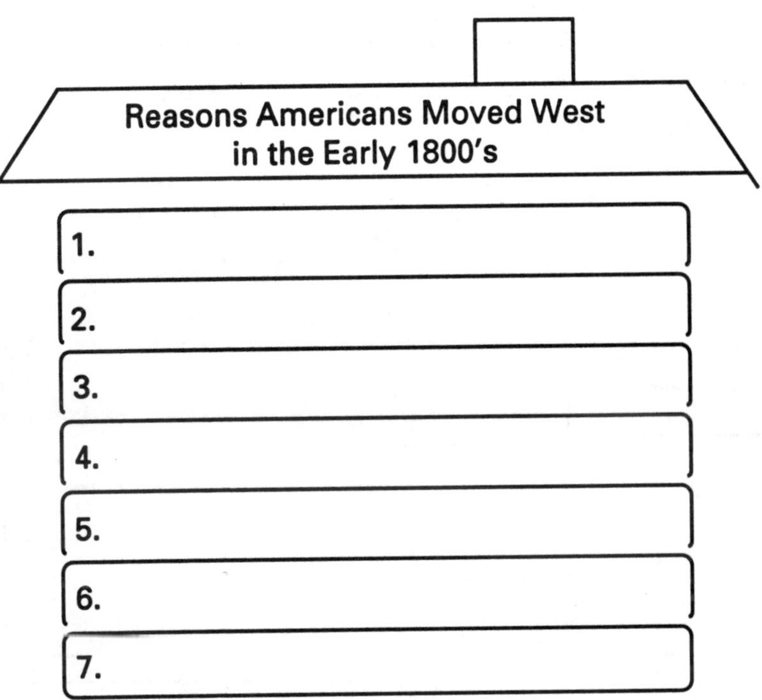

Pictures: Often drawing a picture will help you remember the information. You don't have to be an artist! Your picture should have something to do with the subject of the notes. When you take a test and having trouble remembering, close your eyes and try to visualize the drawing; you have a good chance of also remembering the information that goes with it.

Discussion: This format is good when you take notes from a movie, video, panel of speakers, or class discussion.

___/___/9__

What Was Said

Speaker

Homework Sheet of ______________________

Week of ____ / ____ – ____ / ____ / ____

Doodle Here

Periods

( ) = Parents, Initials

	1	2	3	4	5	6	7
•**Monday** To Do							
•**Tuesday** To Do							
•**Wednesday** To Do							
•**Thursday** To Do							
•**Friday** To Do							

Long-Term Assignments **Due:**

______________________ __/__/__

______________________ __/__/__

Doodle Here

Homework Sheet of ____________________

Week of ___ / ___ – ___ / ___ / ___

Doodle Here

Periods

( ) = Done

	1	2	3	4	5	6	7
•Monday To Do ( )							
•Tuesday To Do ( )							
•Wednesday To Do ( )							
•Thursday To Do ( )							
•Friday To Do ( )							

Long-Term Assignments	**Due:**
____________________	___/___/___
____________________	___/___/___

Doodle Here

Name ______________________

Homework Due Week of ____ / ____ – ____ / ____ / ____

Remember to Do	Date Due

Subjects	Monday	Tuesday	Wednesday	Thursday	Friday
1 ______ Books/Materials Needed					
2 ______ Books/Materials Needed					
3 ______ Books/Materials Needed					
4 ______ Books/Materials Needed					
5 ______ Books/Materials Needed					
Initials of Parents:					

Doodling Space

" Active Listening–An important quote I heard

______________________________________"

____

____
Speaker

Name ______________________

Homework Due Week of ___ / ___ – ___ / ___ / ___

Remember to Do	Date Due

Subjects	Monday	Tuesday	Wednesday	Thursday	Friday
1 ______ Books/Materials Needed					
2 ______ Books/Materials Needed					
3 ______ Books/Materials Needed					
4 ______ Books/Materials Needed					
5 ______ Books/Materials Needed					
✔ when done	☐	☐	☐	☐	☐

Doodling Space

Active Listening—An important quote I heard

"______________________________________

______________________________________"

____
Speaker

Notes about taking notes: Notice that, with each of the samples we gave you, we put the date at the top. Dating any notes is super important if you don't want a mass of running information. You can fill in notes if you miss a day or you can easily refer to the notes of one particular day. Putting a date on everything you do takes little time and is a helpful habit to have.

No matter which way you use to take notes (hopefully, you will come up with your own way, a way that works best for you), use the ideas that we gave you in Chapter 6.

Notes: